The White House
An American Symbol

Alison and Stephen Eldridge

Enslow Elementary

an imprint of

Enslow Publishers, Inc.

40 Industrial Road
Box 398
Berkeley Heights, NJ 07922
USA

http://www.enslow.com

Enslow Elementary, an imprint of Enslow Publishers, Inc.
Enslow Elementary® is a registered trademark of Enslow Publishers, Inc.

Library of Congress Cataloging-in-Publication Data
Eldridge, Alison.
 The White House : an American symbol / by Alison and Stephen Eldridge.
   p. cm.
 Includes index.
 Summary: "Introduces pre-readers to simple concepts about the importance of the White House using
short sentences and repetition of words"—Provided by publisher.
 ISBN 978-0-7660-4062-5
 1. White House (Washington, D.C.)—Juvenile literature. 2. Presidents—United States—Juvenile
literature. 3. Washington (D.C.)—Buildings, structures, etc.—Juvenile literature. I. Eldridge, Stephen.
II. Title.
 F204.W5E43 2012
 975.3—dc23
                                         201102853
Future editions:
Paperback ISBN 978-1-4644-0050-6
ePUB ISBN 978-1-4645-0957-5
PDF ISBN 978-1-4645-0957-2

Printed in China
012012 Leo Paper Group, Heshan City, Guangdong, China
10 9 8 7 6 5 4 3 2 1

To Our Readers: We have done our best to make sure all Internet Addresses in this book were active
and appropriate when we went to press. However, the author and the publisher have no control over and
assume no liability for the material available on those Internet sites or on other Web sites they may link
to. Any comments or suggestions can be sent by e-mail to comments@enslow.com or to the address on
the back cover.

Photo Credits: © 1999 Artville, LLC, pp. 3 (capital), 18–19; Annie Leibovitz/Released by White
House Photo Office, pp. 8–9; © iStockphoto.com/narvikk, p. 22; Official White House Photo by Chuck
Kennedy, pp. 12–13; Official White House Photo by Pete Souza, pp. 3 (president), 6–7, 10, 14–15;
Shutterstock.com, pp. 1, 4–5, 16, 20.

Cover Photo: Shutterstock.com

Note to Parents and Teachers

Help pre-readers get a jump start on reading. These lively stories introduce simple concepts with
repetition of words and short simple sentences. Photos and illustrations fill the pages with color and
effectively enhance the text. Free Educator Guides are available for this series at www.enslow.com.
Search for the *All About American Symbols* series name.

Contents

Words to Know

capital   president

I see the White House.

The president lives
in the White House.

President Barack Obama and his wife, Michelle, have two daughters: Sasha (left) and Malia.

His family lives
there, too.

The White House
has six floors.

It has 132 rooms.

It has 35 bathrooms, too!

The president works in the White House.

He meets with people.
They make laws.

Where do I see the White House?

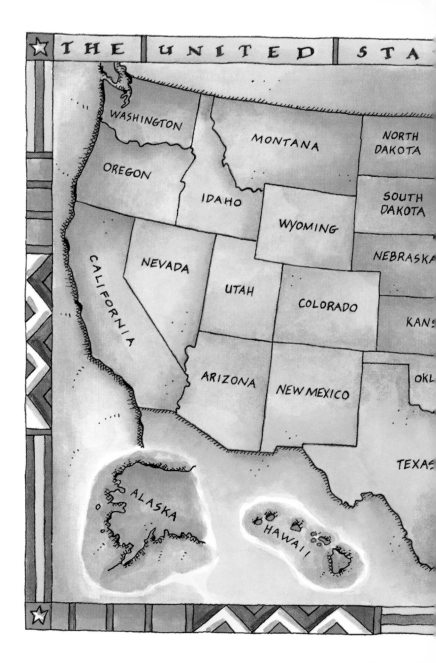

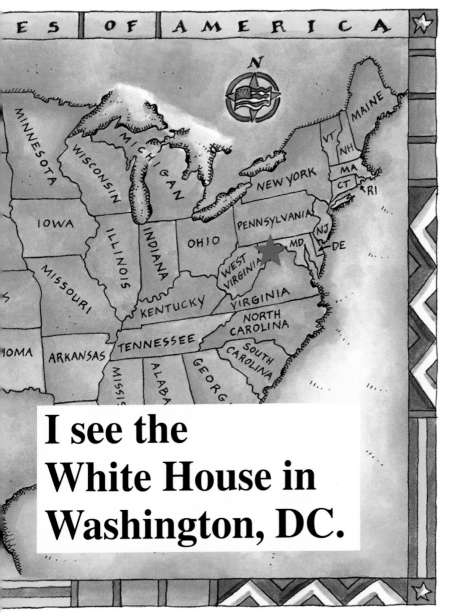

I see the
**White House in
Washington, DC.**

Washington, DC, is the capital of America.

It is the most important city.

I see the White House.

I think of America!

Read More

Ashley, Susan. *The White House*. Milwaukee, Wis.: Weekly Reader Early Learning, 2004.

Marks, Jennifer L. *President Barack Obama*. Mankato, Minn.: Capstone Press, 2009.

Rinaldo, Denise. *White House Q&A*. New York: Collins, 2008.

Web Sites

EnchantedLearning.com. *White House Coloring Printout.* © 2003-2010. <http://www.enchantedlearning.com/history/us/monuments/whitehouse/printout.shtml>

The White House. *Presidential Pets.* <http://www.whitehouse.gov/photos-and-video/photogallery/presidential-pets>

Index

Guided Reading Level: **B**
Guided Reading Leveling System is based on the guidelines recommended by Fountas and Pinnell.

Word Count: **83**